T0144998

How to Attract
the Man of
Your Dreams

A CHRISTIAN WOMAN'S GUIDE
TO SUCCESS IN LOVE

By Patricia Van Pelt, PhD

Entrepreneur, Speaker, Author, Overcomer

Illinois State Senator

WESTBOW
PRESS®
A DIVISION OF THOMAS NELSON
& ZONDERVAN

Copyright © 2017 Patricia Van Pelt, PhD.

All rights reserved. No part of this book may be used
or reproduced by any means, graphic, electronic, or
mechanical, including photocopying, recording, taping or
by any information storage retrieval system without the
written permission of the author except in the case of brief
quotations embodied in critical articles and reviews.

WestBow Press books may be ordered through
booksellers or by contacting:

WestBow Press
A Division of Thomas Nelson & Zondervan
1663 Liberty Drive
Bloomington, IN 47403
www.westbowpress.com
1 (866) 928-1240

Because of the dynamic nature of the Internet, any web
addresses or links contained in this book may have changed
since publication and may no longer be valid. The views
expressed in this work are solely those of the author and do
not necessarily reflect the views of the publisher, and the
publisher hereby disclaims any responsibility for them.

Any people depicted in stock imagery provided
by Thinkstock are models, and such images are
being used for illustrative purposes only.
Certain stock imagery © Thinkstock.

ISBN: 978-1-5127-8610-1 (sc)
ISBN: 978-1-5127-8611-8 (hc)
ISBN: 978-1-5127-8609-5 (e)

Library of Congress Control Number: 2017907450

Print information available on the last page.

WestBow Press rev. date: 7/08/2017

Scripture quotes marked (NCV) are taken from the New Century Version®. Copyright © 2005 by Thomas Nelson. Used by permission. All rights reserved.

Scripture quotations marked (NIV) are taken from the Holy Bible, New International Version®, NIV®. Copyright © 1973, 1978, 1984, 2011 by Biblica, Inc.™ Used by permission of Zondervan. All rights reserved worldwide. *

Scripture quotations are taken from the Holy Bible, New Living Translation, copyright ©1996, 2004, 2007, 2013, 2015 by Tyndale House Foundation. Used by permission of Tyndale House Publishers, Inc., Carol Stream, Illinois 60188. All rights reserved.

Scripture quotes marked (KJV) are taken from the King James Version of the Bible.

Scripture quotations taken from the Amplified® Bible (AMP), Copyright © 2015 by The Lockman Foundation Used by permission. www.Lockman.org

Scripture quotations marked (AMPC) are taken from the Amplified® Bible, Copyright © 1954, 1958, 1962, 1964, 1965, 1987 by The Lockman Foundation Used by permission. www.Lockman.org

*You Are the Dream That Your
Soul Mate Is Having Right Now*

To all of you saved, sanctified, and fire-baptized women of God who have overcome so many of life's challenges but are waiting for the appearance of the man of your dreams—the one God sent.

Preface

This book is designed for the Christian woman who desires to be married to the man of her dreams but is unsure which steps she should take to meet the one man God has for her. This is my open letter to you explaining the revelation that God gave me about attraction and the one He has sent.

Introduction

How to Attract the Man of Your Dreams is for the unmarried Christian woman that is trusting God to reveal her soulmate in His good timing. This book is both for you and about you. The written word and the implications of this book are for spiritual women of God to examine, believe, embrace, and share.

This book is about our lives, our love, our tears, our commitment to walking in the light of God's Word, and our willingness to wait patiently on God, no matter how long it takes.

I want you to recognize how beautiful you are. You are a treasure waiting to be found. Men all over the world are looking for beautiful women who are loyal, loving, spiritual, industrious, wise, compassionate, and forward-thinking. What's more, the Word of God has assigned great value to finding a wife.

> *The man who finds a wife finds a treasure, and he receives favor from the LORD. (Proverbs 18:22, NLT)*

So let your confidence rest on the certainty that your Father will not hold any good thing from you. For you are the dream that your soul mate is having right now!

Are You Curious?

Do you ever wonder why even after you've prayed and prayed, you don't seem to succeed in the areas that mean the most to you? Yet other people with less skill and less spirituality outperform you, make more money than you, find true love and affection, or consistently achieve their powerful goals?

Are you curious about how some find true love while others seem to wander aimlessly?

Are you wondering if you're wasting your life by being too discriminating, while waiting for the man of your dreams to find you?

Have you asked yourself what's missing?

If you answered yes to one or more of these questions, this book was written for you!

You Will Learn

- what it takes to find the person of your dreams;
- how a woman of God should position herself to find success in love;
- how to have an active dating life that fulfills the plan of God; and
- how to be sure he is the one and what to do next.

Now let's journey through the revelation that God has given to His daughters about attraction and the one He sends.

Part One

Chapter 1

Waiting for Love

I wrote this book because God's women are in waiting. I see that familiar look on the faces of Christian women in every church, at social gatherings, and even in the business world. These single women are confident, diligent, loyal, beautiful, and committed, yet they are in waiting. They are waiting for the one God sends.

I, too, waited and waited. I even buried my desire to be married for decades. No matter how I looked at it, there was no explanation for the plight of the single women of God in the church. I just didn't know what to do.

So I turned my face toward God and began to inquire about my circumstances and the plight of single women in the church. If you are like I was back then, you want to move forward but can't find the answers you need to take the next step in your love life.

I found that that there is very little advice on how a woman of God might find true love, other than to just sit and wait for it to happen. I wrote this book based on my experiences and eventual realization that we spend too much time waiting for God to do the things He has called *us* to do, while we attempt to do the things that only *God* can do.

Read this passage of Scripture and believe it, because it is the truth:

> *For I know the thoughts* that I think toward you, saith the LORD, *thoughts* of *peace, and not of evil, to give you an expected end. (Jeremiah 29:11, KJV)*

I know it is God's goal to give us success, so why not success in love? We've all read,

> *"Seek ye first the kingdom of God and his righteousness, and all these things shall be added unto you."* *(Matthews 6:33, KJV)*

Furthermore, the Scriptures state that everything we need, even our heart's desire, will be added to our lives if we delight in Him. I'm sure you believe these Scriptures are true.

I believed—and still do believe—the Word of God. And yet I had no answer whatsoever for the young women who asked why there were so many unmarried women in the church who had given their entire adult lives to God. That question gnawed at me for years.

I knew I had a lot to offer, but it didn't seem that the man of my dreams—my soul mate—could find me.

Based on the following verse, I knew that God had already given me all that I needed to live, love, and thrive.

His divine power hath given unto us all things that pertain unto life and godliness, through the knowledge of Him that hath called us to glory and virtue. (2 Peter 1:3, KJ21)

In addition, I knew it is not God's will to hold any good thing from His people. He promised that if I delighted myself in Him, He would give me the desires of my heart. He seemed to freely give me everything else, so wouldn't he give me a good man, too?

A History of Success

After giving my heart to Christ, I experienced exponential success in every area of my life. So it didn't make sense to me that a good man of God with good intentions had not found me.

Was I too strict? Did I weigh too much? Was I repelling men of God somehow? Every time I thought about this, I simply felt frustrated.

So I buried my desire, which is something you should never do. When men flirted with me, sometimes I didn't realize it. Other times I would flat-out ignore them. I felt I didn't have time to entertain even the idea of a conversation. Anyway, I was sure Satan sent all of them. If God had sent them, I would know it, right?

As days became months, months became years, and years became decades, the chance of meeting and marrying Mr.

Right seemed like just a dream that was fading away.

So I used my time to focus on other things.

Success Across the Board

It didn't take me long to figure out that I could attract everything I needed to succeed. I could monopolize anything I turned my attention toward—that is, except in the area of finding true love.

Education: In spite of being a high school dropout, I returned to school and earned a PhD in management in record time and also received my license as an Illinois certified public accountant.

Politics: Though I had no political experience, I successfully ran for the Illinois State Senate as an outsider and won against all odds. Now I'm gearing up for my third term.

Business: After joining my first network marketing company, I broke every record and hit the coveted position of senior vice president in fifty-nine days, receiving a brand-new 2014 BMW as a reward. Less than a year later, I was promoted to platinum senior vice president and was awarded a 2014 Bentley convertible.

Social justice: Utilizing my studies in social movements, political action, and personal development, I have traveled around the world, speaking and training thousands on various topics related to overcoming social challenges and gaining success.

My spiritual life: The church that started in my house under the leadership of Apostle Joseph L. Stanford grew into a worldwide ministry that afforded me the opportunity to travel the world, preach the gospel, and establish churches based on the principles that we can be one with God and that He wants to have a Father and son relationship with even the least of us.

Through Christ, I found that I could achieve anything I put my mind to. And I had been very successful in every area—almost. I used prayer, meditation, and the power of faith to move mountains out of my way. I preached, prophesied, cast out devils, and prayed for the sick and saw them healed by the power of God. Nothing could stop me from achieving anything that I set my mind to.

But true love continued to elude me.

The enjoyment of experiencing the satisfying love of a soul mate eluded me for decades until I learned some primary truths that pushed past my biases and shortsightedness. Only then did I learn and understand the secrets to attracting the man of my dreams— my soul mate, the one God had for me. I'll never forget how flabbergasted I was when God began to unveil His truth to me.

As you read the chapters that follow, I pray you, too, will clearly understand your role in God's plan and how to attract the best that God has for you. Onward!

Chapter Two

Faith Without Works:
Dead on Arrival

According to 1 Corinthian 2, spiritual things must be discerned spiritually. Otherwise, they make no sense at all. In this chapter, I will share revelation knowledge that I received only because of my history of walking with God.

> *Now we have received, not the spirit of the world, but the spirit, which is of God; that we might know the things that are freely given to us of God. (1 Corinthian 2:12, KJV)*

We know the power of faith very well. Likewise, we know that faith and action operate together to create the outcome we pray for. Let's look at a few commonsense actions that you take every day.

- If you're hungry, you prepare something to eat.
- If you want to be closer to God, you increase your prayer and meditation time.
- If you need more money, you launch a new business venture or seek a better job.
- If you want to look better, you dress up and use all the beauty techniques available to bring out your natural beauty.
- If you want to get healthier, you don't just sit and pray. You change your eating plan and start a workout routine, right?

So why not do the same in love?

Why not do something to attract the very thing you desire most? In 1 Corinthians 7:9, Paul clearly says it's better to marry than to burn. Do our Bible-believing congregations think Paul was speaking only about males?

In the church, we are taught that a man who *finds* a wife, finds a good thing. So we women sit patiently and wait—and wait—and wait. We wait because the Bible makes no mention of a woman working toward attracting a husband— no matter how badly she desires to be married.

Or does it?

What about Esther? She prepared herself to be presented to King Ahasuerus with the goal of attracting his attention—and ultimately his love. She heeded the instruction of the king's chamberlain, who was the keeper of all the women that hoped to be crowned queen.

When it was Esther's turn to go before King Ahasuerus, she wore only what the king's chamberlain, keeper of all women, recommended.

So Esther was taken unto King Ahasuerus into his house royal in the tenth month, which is the month Tebeth, in the seventh year of his reign. The king loved Esther above all the women, and she obtained grace and favour in his sight more

> *than all the virgins; so that he set*
> *the royal crown upon her head, and*
> *made her queen instead of Vashti.*
> *(Esther 2:16–17, KJV)*

Esther, in all of her beauty, mesmerized King Ahasuerus and attracted his love. But what if she hadn't prepared herself? What if she had simply gone to him with no desire to attract his love? Do you think the results would have been the same? I doubt it.

We must never discount the power that God has given women to bring many sons into glory. We have a power that we ignore: a power to win the confidence and the attention of the opposite sex. I'll discuss this in detail a little later in this book.

Meanwhile, consider Ruth's story.

When we read the book of Ruth, we are introduced to the story of Boaz, Ruth the Moabite, and Naomi, her mother-in-law. Clearly Naomi instructed Ruth on how to attract her soul mate.

Naomi, Boaz, and Ruth

Having lost everything, Naomi had nothing left to offer Ruth. Yet Ruth refused to go back to live among her people, the Moabites. Instead she chose to stay with Naomi, vowing to serve Naomi's God, to dwell among Naomi's people, and to even die where Naomi would die.

As it turns out, Naomi's husband had a relative who was a mighty man of wealth named Boaz. He had noticed Ruth as she worked in the fields, but he had not shown any interest in having a love relationship with her. If it had not been for Naomi's intervention, Ruth might have never known the love of Boaz.

As you look closer at Ruth 3, take note that God sent Naomi to intervene on behalf of Ruth so she could marry the man of her dreams. This book is also sent as an intervention for the many faithful women of God that await the man of their dreams—the one God sent.

According to the Scripture, Naomi had made up her mind that it was time for Ruth to be married.

One day Naomi said to Ruth, "My daughter, it's time that I found a permanent home for you, so that you will be provided for. Boaz is a close relative of ours, and he's been very kind by letting you gather grain with his young women. Tonight he will be winnowing barley at the threshing floor. Now do as I tell you—take a bath and put on perfume and dress in your nicest clothes. Then go to the threshing floor, but don't let Boaz see you until he has finished eating and drinking. Be sure to notice where he lies down; then go and uncover his feet and lie down there. He will tell you what to do."

"I will do everything you say," Ruth replied. So she went down to the threshing floor that night and followed the instructions of her mother-in-law.

After Boaz had finished eating and drinking and was in good spirits, he lay down at the far end of the pile of grain and went to sleep. Then Ruth came quietly, uncovered his feet, and lay down. Around midnight Boaz suddenly woke up and turned over. He was surprised to find a woman lying at his feet! "Who are you?" he asked.

"I am your servant Ruth," she replied. "Spread the corner of your covering over me, for you are my family redeemer."

"The LORD BLESS YOU, MY DAUGHTER!" BOAZ EXCLAIMED. "YOU ARE SHOWING EVEN MORE FAMILY LOYALTY NOW THAN YOU DID BEFORE, FOR YOU HAVE NOT GONE AFTER A YOUNGER MAN, WHETHER RICH OR POOR. Now don't worry about a thing, my daughter. I will do what is necessary, for everyone in town knows you are a virtuous woman."

(Ruth 3:1–11, NLT)

"So Boaz took Ruth, and she was his wife: and when he went in unto her,

> *the Lord gave her conception, and she bare a son." (Ruth 4:1,3 NLT)*

Just as Naomi taught Ruth how to win Boaz, God would have you identify with the man of your dreams as well.

God is so in love with you! He built this whole world around us. He gave His only begotten Son to buy us back when we had sold ourselves into sin. God wants us to have the best of the best.

> *"I say this because I know what I am planning for you," says the LORD. "I have good plans for you, not plans to hurt you. I will give you hope and a good future." (Jeremiah 29:11, NCV)*

According to Scripture, it is not good for a man or a woman to dwell alone unless it's his or her calling to do so. If you desire to marry, guess what? God would have you to be married. I knew that was true. But with no instruction and only tradition to follow, I cut myself short of having a meaningful relationship over and over again until I had a powerful encounter with God.

Like Paul, I felt God knock me down and grab my full attention. I will never forget what He showed me in the Scriptures. Though it challenged all my traditional ideas, I had a strong enough relationship with God to know it was the Spirit. It was the Way. Nevertheless, it would take me years to realize how to follow God's instruction on the subject.

Chapter Three

The Revelation

"How long will you waver and hesitate [to return], O you backsliding daughter? For the Lord has created a new thing in the land [of Israel]: a female shall compass (woo, win, and protect) a man."
(Jeremiah 31:22, AMPC)

When I first read the Amplified version of Jeremiah 31:22 some years ago, I didn't understand it. I saw two competing thoughts in one passage of Scripture. First, "how long will you waver and hesitate [to return], O you backsliding daughter?" and, second, "a female shall compass (woo, win, and protect) a man."

Over time, it became clear that I didn't understand it because I was trying to apply a natural interpretation to a spiritual message that God had sent to His chosen people. So I sought God for clarity.

Through God's grace, He brought me into the understanding of what this verse means:

> *How long will you waver and* hesitate [to return], O you backsliding daughter?

God sent this message to the children of Israel because they were vacillating between God and idols. Israel had failed to fully commit to God and was constantly going back and forth between her lovers and her divine husband.

Throughout the Old Testament, we see God calling the children of Israel to align with His ways and His thoughts so they could enjoy the good of the land that God had promised them. So the term "backsliding daughters" didn't rankle me. I understood that part.

But what followed was astonishing:

> *"For the Lord has created a new thing in the land of Israel: a female shall compass (woo, win, and protect) a man."*

I must say I was shocked. I had so many questions. What's more, at first glance, the verse seemed to be contrary to the Scriptures I had been reading for the last three decades. I didn't know what to think or even how a woman of God might apply it in these days.

Clearly God had declared, "I have created a new thing." That new thing required that a woman take the role of protector of the man in her life. This role was not to be obtained by force or rule, but by wooing him and winning his confidence, trust, and respect to such a level that he would allow himself to be led and ultimately protected by her. This is the Lord's doing!

Even with all of this, I was still flabbergasted. *Me? An evangelist, woo a man? Oh my God! But I am a woman of God.* I had never dreamt of doing such a thing. It was contrary to all my natural inclinations.

To me, wooing was something that a loose woman might do. And isn't the man supposed to woo and win the love of the woman? And what does this whole thing about protection mean? I am the weaker vessel, right? Doesn't that mean the man is supposed to protect me?

With all these questions clouding my mind, I knew God was challenging me to see His vision for my future—a vision so far removed from everything I had been taught and had believed for more than three decades. Yet I knew it was God.

That's when I took the blinders off and took the time to look through a spiritual lens. From that vantage point, it was clear that women in the Bible were power players, just as we are today in churches across the world. Yes, men were in charge. But in many instances, it was the women who—though they held untitled positions—wielded substantial power behind closed doors. Women have carried the church.

Women get that power not because of pity or a commandment. We get it because we position ourselves to serve, and we work hard to protect our churches. We gain the trust of the leaders, and with that trust, we are ushered into a powerful position to guide and protect souls in the house of our God.

The point I'm driving at is this: the actions that put women in positions of power and sustained the church for over two thousand years need to be brought outside the four walls of the church and into the marketplace, where so many men languish.

God's women have a role to play in restoring the path for men to come back into the shepherd's fold. If we sit on our hands and continue to watch the denigration of our men, woe to us. We have a calling to fulfill, and it includes our active role in protecting the men in our lives and those we meet. Does this seem far-fetched to you? Consider this:

> *For by means of a whorish woman a man is brought to a piece of bread: and the adulteress will hunt for the precious life. (Proverbs 6:26, KJV)*

If a woman can bring a man so low that he's compared to nothing more than a piece of bread, why wouldn't she also have the power to protect him? Doesn't this make sense?

And to protect a man, you must first gain his trust. How do you win the trust of an individual? By showing genuine care and concern, by courting and pursuing, by cultivating the relationship, and by seeking to persuade him to do something that is morally right. This is the very definition of *woo*. In its simplest form, *woo* means to make someone like you. We win their trust by wooing—by seeking their favor, affection, respect, and love.

There are many definitions of *woo*—from courting to cultivating. Let's focus on the definition of *woo* from Dictionary.com:

woo (verb)

1. To seek the favor, affection, or love of, especially with a view to marriage;
2. To seek to win;
3. To invite (consequences, whether good or bad) by one's own action;
4. To seek to persuade (a person, group, etc.), as to do something; solicit; importune.

Yes, we must woo. We must win. And we must protect. God has dismissed the traditional role of women. He is calling for women to take responsibility for protecting our men—that is, our sons, nephews, uncles, brothers, fathers, husbands, and yes, even those men that God causes to cross our path.

The prophetic words that my pastor, Apostle Joseph L. Stanford, spoke over my life ring true: "Abraham wanted a son. But God wanted a nation. Both were accomplished as Abraham walked in agreement with God. As the promise was with Abraham, so it is with you. Walk in agreement with God, and all of the desires of your heart will be yours." Amen!

Let's walk in agreement with God. So many of our men are drifting aimlessly through life—disconnected from

God, disconnected from purpose, and disconnected from the church. According to the will and plan of God, we have a power within us to woo, win, and protect the men that God causes to come into our lives. Let's use it!

God Calls for Women

When trouble struck the land, God said, "Send for the women who are skilled with bringing us before God with a repentant heart."

This is what the LORD ALMIGHTY SAYS:
"Consider now! Call for the
wailing women to come;
send for the most skillful of them.

Let them come quickly
and wail over us
till our eyes overflow with tears
and water streams from our eyelids."
(Jeremiah 9:17–18, NIV)

"For death is come up into our
windows, and is entered into our
palaces, to cut off the children
from without, and the young
men from the streets."
(Jeremiah 9:21, **KJV**)

God said to send for the women who are
skillful in causing us to get to the place
of repentance that will save our lives.
These skillful women do not come in
with a fire hose and spray down every
man with the Bible. They come in with
wisdom, care, and persuasion. They are

trustworthy and without judgment. And through their actions, they bring men to a place of repentance.

When we understand our role in bringing many sons to God, we learn how to use the power that God has given us as women.

According to the Word of God, he who wins souls is wise. Those of us who are wise will learn the art of wooing. We will practice it and learn to win the trust and respect of the men who cross our path. And we will become the ones that protect our men by the grace and power of our Father.

If you are looking for more on the subject, I suggest you look to the Word of God.

- Rahab, a prostitute who lived in Jericho, used her ability to woo, win, and protect the Hebrews that had come to spy out the land. Later she married an Israelite and became an ancestor of Jesus Christ.
- Abigail, a wise woman, won David's confidence and thereby protected Nabal from being slaughtered by David and his men. Abigail was so convincing that David loved her and took her as his wife after Nabal died.
- Moses's mother protected her son in spite of the king's murderous ambition.

How many times have you sought to protect the men in your life? Yes, God is doing a new thing in the earth. A woman shall woo, win, and protect a man.

In your righteous role, you will bring many sons into the knowledge of who God is and what His calling means for them. In the process, you will exponentially increase your chances of catching the eye of the man who is already dreaming about you.

As Apostle Stanford said, Abraham wanted a son, but God wanted a nation. Both were accomplished as Abraham walked in agreement with God, even though what God commanded was not traditional. Are you ready?

Part 2

In the upcoming chapters, I share five steps for attracting the man of your dreams. But before we start, I want to make sure you are equipped to succeed in recognizing the type of man who will be your soul mate.

To help with this process, I will share the outline of a book I recently wrote, *The 7 Critical Steps to Success*. The book covers the most important steps you might take to achieve true success. The steps and process are as follows:

1. Ambition—the desire to succeed. You must have ambition to achieve any goal, whether it's finishing school, getting your business off the ground, or attracting your soul mate—the man of your dreams.

2. Vision—the act or the power to anticipate what will be. Without a vision, people lose hope and perish, and so it is with you. Therefore, it is important that you begin to envision yourself as being successful in meeting and recognizing your soul mate.

3. Belief—the acceptance that something is true or that something exists. Belief is absolutely necessary. You cannot allow yourself to be double-minded. Either you believe

your soul mate exists or you don't. Make this declaration early. Otherwise, you won't be able to take this revelation for your own life. Nor will you have the power to teach others.

4. Roadmap—a detailed plan to guide progress to *your* goal. You will create a five-step plan later in this book.

5. Resolve—a definite and earnest decision about something and being dogged about it. Ask yourself if you're really ready to learn how to attract the man of your dreams? Are you really ready to take this journey? Once you come to a place of resolve, no one and nothing will be powerful enough to stop you.

6. Faith—having complete confidence and trust. Do you have confidence that God will be able to bring your soul mate into your life? Do you believe God will bring you into the place where you will have everything that pertains to life and godliness? Do you have faith that God will give you the wisdom required to woo, win, and protect His sons?

7. Personal and professional growth—what got you here won't get you there. In other words, what got you inspired enough to pick up this book is good. But to receive all that awaits you, you must grow up in God. You must receive wisdom, knowledge, and fresh oil from

heaven to refresh and reignite you for the journey you're about to take. This means a commitment to personal growth and spiritual development. You need to know more, and you must trust God to get you to the land of promise.

As mentioned earlier, Abraham wanted a son, but God wanted a nation. Both were accomplished as Abraham walked faithfully in the manifested plan of God. Sometimes our desire is the very thing God will use to accomplish His ultimate goal, which is to bring many sons into glory. The rest of this book contains the five steps to attracting the man of your dreams. Onward!

Chapter Four

Step 1: Know You!

At the start of this book, I asked my beloved husband, Gene F. Scott, Jr., if he would contribute to this book one way a woman might attract the man of her dreams. He obliged with these words of wisdom:

> *Be yourself at all times, so you never have to become someone else to keep the person you attract. You want to keep him loving you, not a fictitious person you conjured up that day. You really have to be true to yourself.*

This is a very important point to remember. To be yourself, you first must know yourself. It's amazing how many people do not know who they really are. They can clearly see others, but they see themselves through an obscured lens. Therefore, they have a flawed vision of themselves.

When a woman does not know herself, it is almost impossible for her to define what is true. Attracting your soul mate—the one that God sends—requires knowing yourself. In his book *The Art of War*, Sun Tzu explained the peril of not knowing oneself in a time of war:

> If you know the enemy and know yourself, you need not fear the result of a hundred battles. If you know yourself but not the enemy, for every victory gained you will also suffer a defeat. If you know

neither the enemy nor yourself, you will succumb in every battle.

Do You Know You?

Have you spent time watching yourself, analyzing yourself, and being honest about yourself? This isn't about being perfect in your own eyes; it's about knowing yourself and improving or accepting who you are.

Getting to know yourself is priceless, because it gives you guidance when choosing your friends and ultimately attracting your soul mate. In addition, knowing yourself is key when contemplating your career choices and determining which options are likely to lead to success, spiritual growth, and contentment. Moreover, you alone govern all your relationships, so it's very valuable to know who you are. A woman who truly knows herself is wise.

It may seem that it's simple to know yourself and that knowing yourself comes automatically with age, but it doesn't.

The book Job said it best:

> Those [who are] abundant in years may not [always] be wise, nor may the elders [always] understand justice. (Job 32:9, AMP)

Getting to know yourself takes maturity, humility, and responsibility. I believe it's virtually impossible to even recognize the man of your dreams without knowing who you are first.

Finally, knowing yourself is a journey. All of us are becoming more like the Father or less like Him. None of us is standing still; we are all becoming. We should examine ourselves and take note of who we are becoming.

A good friend was going off about how she planned to get back at a person she felt had done her wrong. She saw him as her enemy, and she planned to repay him with a vengeance. While I told her that her attitude was not aligned with the Word of God, she said, "I can't fake what I don't feel. This is just who I am."

I said, "No, this is *not* who you are. This is who you are becoming!"

We are all becoming every moment of our lives. But who are we becoming?

As the great artist Leonardo Da Vinci was working toward fulfilling his commission to paint a portrait of the Last Supper, he knew he wanted the finished product to look as authentic as possible. So he interviewed hundreds of men from which he would select the models for the twelve apostles and the Christ.

Within weeks, he found the perfect Jesus—a gentle and humble man who walked with a sense of power and authority, untouched by sin and immorality. He was youthful and had a light in his eyes that reflected a sense of peace.

About a year later, Da Vinci found the perfect Peter—a robust, quick-tempered man with fire in his eyes and an air of pride and self-confidence. Next he found a man who had the facial features and temperament that he imagined John the beloved had.

Over the next three or four years, Da Vinci found and painted James, Thaddeus, and all the other disciples except one—Judas. He searched and searched for the perfect model to pose as Judas, but all of his searching was to no avail. Being pressured by his benefactor, the duke of Milan, to finish the painting, the artist explained his dilemma to a friend, one of the king's knights. The knight suggested that Da

Vinci interview some of the prisoners under his care.

For nearly seven years, the artist had searched for a man who had the facial expression, spirit, and personality of the Judas he imagined. The artist was shocked when he laid eyes on one particular prisoner—a cold, callous, and unrepentant man with dark, shady eyes that told a story of betrayal. The prisoner was awaiting execution for murder. In his eyes was the exact look of the Judas that Da Vinci had imagined.

With surety that the prisoner was the perfect match, Da Vinci requested that the man be allowed to pose for the final character in what would become one of his most famous paintings. With permission from the king, the prisoner was transported.

As he was led in shackles into the artist's studio, the prisoner recognized the surroundings. Being puzzled that Da Vinci seemed to have no clue who he was, the prisoner asked, "Do you know me? Do you remember me?"

The prisoner did not look at all familiar to the artist. Being engrossed in his work, Da Vinci simply said, "I can't be sure. I've created countless paintings of men."

Pressing more, the prisoner said, "I have been here in this studio, and you paid me to model for a portrait."

Da Vinci was becoming impatient. "You are mistaken. I would have remembered your face."

After that response, the prisoner held his peace. It would take nearly six months for the artist to complete the portrait of Judas. After the last brushstroke, he called for the guard to take the prisoner away.

As the guard shackled him and led him toward the door, the prisoner, knowing that the time of his execution was just days away and that he would not see Da Vinci again, turned angrily toward the artist and said, "How could you not remember me? You claim to be a great artist, yet you don't even recognize your subjects. Some years back, I posed for a portrait right here in this same studio."

The artist said, "You are mistaken. I spend much time creating my paintings, which means I spend much time with my models. I am definitely able to recognize all of the men and women that have ever posed for my portraits."

At that point, the prisoner revealed the unbelievable truth. "Sir, I was here. You spent nearly six months completing what you said would be a masterpiece. And now you don't recognize me? How could you not recognize me? Sir, seven years ago, I was your Jesus."

The artist was stunned. The beauty and purity he'd seen in the young man who had posed as his Jesus seven years before was nowhere to be found in the dark, hard face of the man who stood before him.

The prisoner saw himself as looking the same as he had seven years prior. But he had transformed from the perfect image of Jesus to the putrefied image of Judas in seven short years.

We all need assistance if we are to grow into who God is calling us to be. Without having directions and guides to keep us on the track, any of us can become someone else without even recognizing that we are changing.

Learning You

The benefits of knowing *you* cannot be refuted. When you know yourself, you can avoid all types of snares, stumbling blocks, and traps of the enemy. A quick check online reveals that there are numerous assessments, blogs, books, and presentations that can help you identify your key characteristics, values, beliefs, wants, likes, dislikes, strengths, weaknesses, etc.—all of which are a part of who you have become. But to really get down to the essence of who you have become, I recommend taking a values assessment.

Our values change as we develop, grow, and learn. So the exercise below should provide timely insight into yourself. In the list, put an asterisk to the left of up to thirty of your top values.

Accountability	Expertise	Positivity
Accuracy	Exploration	Practicality
Achievement	Expressiveness	Preparedness
Adventurousness	Fairness	Professionalism
Altruism	Faith	Prudence
Ambition	Family-orientation	Quality-orientation
Assertiveness	Fidelity	Reliability
Balance	Fitness	Resourcefulness
Being the best	Fluency	Restraint
Belonging	Focus	Results-oriented
Boldness	Freedom	Rigor
Calmness	Fun	Security
Carefulness	Generosity	Self-actualization
Challenge	Goodness	Self-control
Cheerfulness	Grace	Selflessness
Clear-mindedness	Growth	Self-reliance
Commitment	Happiness	Sensitivity
Community	Hard Work	Serenity
Compassion	Health	Service
Competitiveness	Helping Society	Shrewdness
Consistency	Holiness	Simplicity
Contentment	Honesty	Soundness
Continuous	Honor	Speed
Contribution	Humility	Spirituality
Control	Independence	Spontaneity
Cooperation	Ingenuity	Stability
Correctness	Inner Harmony	Strategic
Courtesy	Inquisitiveness	Strength
Creativity	Insightfulness	Structure
Curiosity	Intelligence	Success
Decisiveness	Intellectual Status	Support
Democraticness		

Dependability	Intuition	Teamwork
Determination	Joy	Temperance
Devoutness	Justice	Thankfulness
Diligence	Leadership	Thoroughness
Discipline	Legacy	Thoughtfulness
Discretion	Love	Timeliness
Diversity	Loyalty	Tolerance
Dynamism	Making a difference	Traditionalism
Economy	Mastery	Trustworthiness
Effectiveness	Merit	Truth-seeking
Efficiency	Obedience	Understanding
Elegance	Openness	Uniqueness
Empathy	Order	Unity
Enjoyment	Originality	Usefulness
Enthusiasm	Patriotism	Vision
Equality	Perfection	Vitality
Excellence	Personal Growth	Wealth
Excitement	Piety	Winning

From the thirty, put a small mark next to ten that best capture what you value most.

Now narrow the ten down further by circling only the top three. These three should reflect what you value above everything else. They should be what you are willing to fight for and, if necessary, die for.

Write down the three values and answer the questions about each of them below.

Value #1

Why is this value important?

What have you done or been willing to do to protect this value in the past?

Value #2

Why is this value important?

What have you done or been willing to do to protect this value in the past?

Value #3

Why is this value important?

What have you done or been willing to do to protect this value in the past?

Did you learn something about yourself?

If you are an authentic person, you will find that your heart's desire, spiritual purpose, and life goals all tie back to your values. If not, don't fret, because it simply means you are still on the journey of learning who you are, which is fine.

Your values are especially important when determining whether the person you meet is your life partner—the man of your dreams, the one God sent.

After knowing yourself, you can choose either to improve or to accept who you are. That's for you to decide. If you decide you need to become better, consider getting help from some of those who are closest to you.

Who Do Men Say You Are?

When Jesus asked the question, "Who do you say I am?" He didn't ask it of people who hadn't spent time with him. Neither should you. Talk to your pastor, spiritually-minded friends, and family members who love you dearly.

Get help by asking them to be your confidantes as you struggle to get better in the areas that are important for your growth. If you want to become your best self, be open to suggestions and insights, especially from those who love you.

Remember, when working to become your best self, never underestimate your greatest teacher—the Holy Spirit.

"Howbeit when he, the Spirit of truth, is come, he will guide you into all truth: for he shall not speak of himself; but whatsoever he shall hear, that shall he speak and he will shew you things to come." (John 16:13, KJV)

Becoming Your Best Self

For as he thinketh in his heart, so is he: Eat and drink, saith he to thee; but his heart is not with thee. (Proverbs 23:7, KJV)

Don't shortchange yourself as you strive to become your best self. Remember, according to the book of Genesis, we are made in the image and likeness of God. We have the capacity and intellect to build, create, develop, and become what we need to become in order to adapt to, challenge, and/or subdue our environment. Never surrender to your lower self's desires, like vengeance, wrath, rage, and such.

As you read earlier, when confronted with the fact that her plans weren't aligned with the Word of God, my good friend said, "This is just who I am!" Sometimes we think we are just who we are, but nothing is further from the truth. Every day we are becoming. And what we are becoming is what we can expect a potential life partner to see.

Chapter Five

Step 2: Know What You Want and Need

Therefore a man shall leave his father and his mother and shall become united *and* cleave to his *wife, and they shall become one flesh. (Genesis 2:24, AMPC)*

The Word of God is so plain and clear that it causes many who are wise to stumble over its simplicity. I'm sure you've seen examples of this truth many times. So let's confront that issue here.

If a man is to leave his mother and father and become one with his wife, wouldn't it be important that he and his would-be wife be on equal footing educationally, physically, financially, spiritually, etc.?

So how do we deal with that when so many women of color seem to outstrip their counterparts in all of these areas? To solve this quandary, I point to the Word.

> *Be ye not unequally yoked together with unbelievers: for what fellowship hath righteousness with unrighteousness? and what communion hath light with darkness? (2 Corinthians 6:14, KJV)*

Truly education, financial status, etc., are important, but none of these should be at the top of your list. According to the Word, the most important thing is that he be a believer. If he is a believer and is willing to hear you, you will be able to help each other grow in many areas.

Growing Up

When considering whom you need or want as a life partner, you must not only examine your prospects but also put the spotlight on yourself. Realize that every time you cross the threshold of a new relationship, you bring you with you. You are the only constant. So the question of who you are or your life's purpose is of utmost importance— especially since you will be bringing yourself to every date, meeting, chance encounter, and ultimately to the altar, if that's God's will.

Along with examining your values, loved ones' input, and the direction of the Holy Spirit, ask yourself the following questions:

- Am I ready to walk in unity with the man of my dreams?
- Are there areas in my life that I need to bring before the throne of God so I can get help?
- Am I in a good place for me— mentally, emotionally, physically, and spiritually?
- Can I count on me to stand for the truth, or am I wishy-washy?

You need to be on a path to a good place when you meet your soul mate, knowing that you both will bring out the best in each other. If you're not there, rest assured that the world does not end here.

God's love for you is greater than your shortcomings, weaknesses, and sins. He will guide you to the place where your best self can emerge, and He will be glorified in the process.

The Way to God

You must be diligent in your commitment to trust God to make you whole. Start by being grateful to God for all He has done already. Believe me, He has done much more than you imagine. In addition, research shows that growing in gratitude is directly tied to life satisfaction and soul peace, which are attractive and valuable in relationship building.

Next ask God to give you a heart of mercy and empathy for those called by Him. If you tend to attract the wrong types of guys, ask God to help you care about what He cares about.

As my husband says, the last thing a man wants is a woman who is not whole and is expecting her man to fix her. Likewise, do not think it is your role to fix the men in your life. That is God's work, and even He requires a personal commitment.

To keep working toward repairing someone who can be healed only through spiritual journeying and a personal commitment to growth is to ask yourself to come to a standstill in your own spiritual and emotional journey, which is not God's will. So ask God to help you love what He loves.

Healing Comes from God

Jesus said that healing is the children's bread. He will heal all who come to Him. So your role—in wooing and winning—is to help men find their way to God—not to be the way.

There's nothing wrong with desiring a mate who you can help move forward in finding his purpose. But if the strain of it causes you to vacillate between trusting God and leaving Him, go with

God. You cannot expect that it would be God's will for you to be locked up with that man for the rest of your life.

Two people will not walk together unless they have agreed to do so. (Amos 3:3, NCV)

Wanting what you refuse to become is error. So you are the Prince Charming in this situation, because you have the power to woo; you have the power to win; and you have the power to protect.

Know What You Want in a Relationship

Are you interested in a builder or a domesticator? A homebody or a busybody? An entrepreneur or an employee? Are you in the upward-mobility season of your life, or are you coming in for a landing? Once you're sure of what you need and want, it will be much simpler to recognize your soul mate.

The Bible states that if we delight ourselves in God, he will give us our heart's desire. However, if you aren't sure what your heart's desire is, you won't even recognize it if He gives it to you. A double-minded woman is woefully unstable in all her ways, so be sure about what you need for your work and your purpose to be fulfilled.

The man of your dreams is waiting, and he is looking for the woman he has known only in his dreams. So, the question becomes, "Are you the woman of his dreams? What kind of woman would the man of your dreams be attracted to? And are you ready?"

Chapter Six

Step 3: Be Where He Will Be

The last thing you want to do is to project an ideal man into your future who you will never be in a position to meet. Therefore, *being where he will be* is one of the most important steps for the spiritual woman seeking success in love. So take special note of all that follows.

Where is the man of your dreams right now? What does he think about? What does he spend his time doing? What are his values? And what drives him? More importantly, who are you, and do you do or say what will bridge your relationship from a casual hello to something infinitely more?

Any day that you walk out of the house could be the day you meet the man of your dreams. Whether you can connect with him or not will be determined by where you dwell emotionally, spiritually, and naturally.

You might just get one glimpse of a chance to connect, so let's focus on the things that matter.

Live in Your Successful Life Now

Once you've determined your life ambition, stay on track by using the seven critical steps to success mentioned in chapter 2. From there, you can envision the type of man you want to attract. Once you get through the visioning stage, you'll know clearly which relationships are worth pursuing and which are not.

Moving the Ball Forward

If you want a life partner who is successful, be around people who have the spirit, values, and wealth mindset that you desire in a mate. Analyze your closest relationships to determine whether they add value to your life or not. Jim Rohn, an excellent personal development master, teaches that your life achievements, weight, physical health, financial wherewithal, and educational and societal status reflect the average of the sum total of the five people with whom you spend the most time. The Scriptures confirm that point as well.

> *Do not be so deceived and misled! Evil companionships (communion, associations) corrupt and deprave good manners and morals and character. (1 Corinthians 15:33, AMPC)*

So walk with those that have achieved what you want to achieve or are at least going where you plan to go. If you don't know people of that caliber, buy books and attend seminars and conferences that focus on success and personal development. Flood your mind with the thoughts, words, and actions of the truly successful, and learn their way so you can live that way.

Walk in the Spirit of Who You Are

Be present and ready to share words of gratitude, positivity, and grace with the people you meet. Don't walk around aimlessly and mindlessly, as if you have nothing to offer. You can give everyone a warm hello or a thank-you with a smile. But go further, ask God to give you wit and wisdom so you know how to speak in such a way that you attract hearers.

I know a young woman who always shouted insults at men who offered her compliments. When I asked her why she would do such a thing, she said she was a married woman so they had no business saying anything to her.

I'm not going to waste a lot of time telling you that you can't win people over if you're hurling insults at them. That's obvious. What I will tell you is not to fear a compliment. Some men don't know how to start a conversation, so their opening remark might not hit the top of the chart on your man-of-my-dreams meter. But that's okay. Give him a break. Men get rejected over and over again by women. They're just trying to be acknowledged. Believe it or not, many men have a terrible fear of rejection. This fear silences many of the very men God desires to bring into the knowledge of His kingdom.

So don't be one of those rejecters. Be ready to speak something of value to everyone, and keep in mind that you can also start the conversation.

Wear a smile. Be sure your hair, nails, and clothing are looking good. And take a note from Naomi: put on some perfume.

Let the words of your mouth and the meditations of your heart always reflect the caliber of woman that you are. Keep in mind that men say there's something really sexy about a woman who walks with poise and confidence. As you stay in that vein, you will be what your dream man is dreaming about.

And just as you will recognize him, he will recognize you.

Chapter Seven

Step 4: Are You in a Position to Be Found?

He who finds a [true and faithful] wife finds a good thing. And obtains favor and approval from the LORD. (Proverbs 18:22, AMP)

When I was sure I wanted to be married, like any good strategist, I began to assess my possibilities for meeting Mr. Right. My social life was nonexistent, and I worked night and day. So I knew I was relegated to meeting Mr. Right either at church or in my work as a state senator. At first glance, both promised to be fertile ground for a woman who desired to be married.

I say "at first glance" because our church had regular fellowship with seven or eight other churches. So we were always visiting churches and meeting new people. In those days, all the women married men who were members of one of the churches. But like I said, that was the past. Over the last twenty years, the church has been increasingly filled with women and children. Very few men attend. (Could this be the result of women failing to woo?) In addition, we don't visit other churches like we did in the old days.

Thus my choices were limited to those who came into the church building. And of course, there were twenty women there to every male. As I perused my options, I quickly saw the downside of limiting my expectation of meeting my soul mate only at the church. That was disappointing, to say the least.

As I looked at the possibilities of meeting Mr. Right during the course of my work, I noted that there were plenty of professional men who frequent the state capitol as lobbyists, lawmakers, businessmen, constituents, and public officials.

But as a senator, when I meet with people, I'm usually in the position of power. Few men have the courage to approach me—or any other female senator—for fear of it not going well and the awkwardness that might follow.

So I decided it only made sense to go where men were looking for a wife. And that meant going online.

Online?!

I still remember the responses of those closest to me when I announced I had met someone on an online dating site. My mom was on board from the beginning, wanting to be kept abreast of every contact and watching anxiously to see what would come of each interaction. In fact, she was my biggest cheerleader.

Unfortunately she was in the minority. From everyone other than my mom, all I got were disapproving looks followed by a gasp, "Oh no!" and "What in the world?"

My son said, "Mom, what about God? What happened to waiting on God?"

A friend and first lady at a church said, "I just think you should give God more time."

Others said, "Evangelist, is that God?" and "What will people say?"

My pastor—though he didn't condemn the tactic—was very leery about the idea. I asked him if he believed that a man who finds a wife finds a good thing. Of course, he said yes. So I asked him if he thought that a woman who wants to be married should go to a place where men are looking for a wife. He affirmed that point as well. I explained to him that, for that purpose, I was going online.

Then I proceeded to share my philosophy about online dating so he could understand how I approached each interaction as well as all the precautions I had taken. He reluctantly supported me. I was very grateful, because I really wanted his support.

As I entered the foray of online dating, I knew I had two things going for me: (1) I could trust myself to date the opposite sex; and (2) I could trust my God to give me the right words. So I prayed and went for it.

At the start, it was overwhelming. It seemed like men were coming from everywhere on the site—white, black, Asian, Muslim, Christian—and that was a lot for me to deal with. Some of the pictures showed men underwater, in caves, on mountains, on bikes, on horses, on boats, on camels. It was way too much. But I didn't give up, and eventually, I figured it out.

Within the first month, I met a nice gentleman from New Jersey. He and I were perfect on paper, and we loved talking to each other—in the beginning. He came to Chicago to visit, and a group of us went out together. It was a great first in-person date, and we had an immediate connection.

But eventually distance and life issues got in our way. He opened a furniture store, and I had to run for office because my term was coming to an end. So our relationship began to wane.

I continued to do research on love relationships, and I branched out to other sites, but just as a bystander. After about five months, I joined another online dating site. But this time, I narrowed my search to just black educated men that didn't smoke, were making at least $75,000, and didn't live in Chicago.

I was on the online dating website for less than a month when I met Gene, my soul mate and the man who would become my husband—the man of my dreams. Both of us had been on the site for less than a month when we met. On the first date, there were little to no fireworks going off, but we were intrigued with each other. So we set a second date. Meanwhile, we talked on the phone, learning more and more about one another. Then the third date came and went.

By then, we were both feeling a connection. But we hadn't defined whether it was a friendship, a business relationship, or something more. At that point, we just let the relationship go where it was going, because we knew we enjoyed being with each other.

What happened over the next few dates took us both by surprise. We had no idea that we would become so deeply connected, develop such a strong love, and care for one another. Neither of us could explain what was happening within us nor express in words the powerful draw that connected us.

All we knew was that we needed each other, and we wanted to be with each other not for hours or days, but forever. He felt that he had a calling to help me achieve all I was called to do. I felt I had a calling to care for him and give him all the love I had stored up for decades.

We married a few months later. I will share more about this in the future, but this story leads to the final step.

Here's an excerpt from the playbook of Warren Buffett, the second richest man in America: "When you see an opportunity and determine it is the right deal and the right time, don't blink!"

Chapter Eight

Step 5: Don't Blink!

And being not weak in faith, he considered not his own body now dead, He staggered not at the promise of God through unbelief; but was strong in faith, giving glory to God; and being fully persuaded that, what he had promised, he was able also to perform. (Romans 4:19–21, JV)

"Don't blink!" is the final step. Abraham understood that it was the will of the Lord for him to have a son. It didn't matter that his wife was too old to have children. Nor was he concerned that his body was no longer responding.

He was fully persuaded that what God promised, He would do.

You have to hold on to that level of faith as well. We have a great cloud of witnesses who have overcome many challenges and have received the benefits of their faith. So have faith. It works.

When you see the right man with the right temperament and right calling, don't waste time playing games. And whatever you do, don't get locked into traditions or ceremonialism. God wants to give each of us our heart's desire, so don't wallow in unbelief, and don't put God on a timeline.

On another note, please know that your soul mate may not be the most handsome man you've ever seen. Don't discount a man because of his outer image. Focus on the inner man. Uncover his purpose, drive, and commitment to spiritual growth. These are the things you will have to live with long after beauty fades.

Check out the wisdom of James Allen in this excerpt from *As a Man Thinketh*:

> Man is made or unmade by himself; in the armory of thought he forges the weapons by which he destroys himself; he also fashions the tools with which he builds for himself heavenly mansions of joy and strength and peace. By the right choice and true application of thought, man ascends to the

Divine Perfection; by the abuse and wrong application of thought, he descends below the level of the beast. Between these two extremes are all the grades of character, and man is their maker and master.

Our men need our faith, love, guidance, and wisdom in order to find their way. We see this dire need in communities, churches, and our homes. Yet there is a deficiency in society that God has called men to fill.

So let's take our rightful role. Let's woo, win, and protect. God has created a new thing: a woman shall encompass a man.

The women that learn to fill this role well are the most beautiful sight a man could ever lay eyes on. So start believing it now, and start accepting and expecting to see your heart's desire.

Many people stumble when it comes to commitment, or they linger in relationships that are noncommittal. Both of these extremes are a waste of your precious life. Choose to trust God and move forward with your life.

Delight yourself in the Lord, and He will give you your heart's desire. God gave His son's life and blood to buy us back. Based on that alone, you can rest assured that He will not hold any good thing from you. God's will is for you to be happy, healed, and prosperous.

If the desire of your heart is to marry the man of your dreams, so be it! Amen!

Take the five steps outlined in this book:

1. Know you.
2. Know what you want and need in a partner.
3. Be where he will be intellectually and spiritually.
4. Be positioned to meet him.
5. When you see him, don't blink!

Now go forth to finish the work that God sent you to do!

Printed in the United States
By Bookmasters